Petals of Wisdom from Grandma

Lorraine Strohbehn

Copyright © 2016 Brenda Strohbehn and Lorraine Strohbehn

Cover photo: Brenda Strohbehn, with special thanks to Janice Goss for the beautiful amaryllis plants

Published via PEP Writing Services through BrendaStrohbehn.com

All rights reserved.

No portion of this material may be reproduced or distributed without the written permission of Brenda Strohbehn, and/or Lorraine Strohbehn, and/or their legal representative(s). Brief portions may be quoted for review purposes.

All Scripture quotations are taken from the King James Version, which is in the public domain.

ISBN: 1530339545
ISBN-13: 978-1530339549

To the memory of my husband, Dr. Ben Strohbehn,
and to our children, grandchildren,
and great-grandchildren

CONTENTS

Acknowledgment i

Around My Kitchen Table 1

Biblical Self Image 33

Choices 53

Death of a Dream 79

About the Author 99

ACKNOWLEDGMENT

With thanks to my daughter Brenda for assisting me in revising and updating these four previously published "letter books."

AROUND MY KITCHEN TABLE

Do you have a nerve center in your home—a place where you are most comfortable with your everyday activities? In our home, that place is my kitchen table. Many family memories are rooted there. Decisions that had life-changing effects were fused at the kitchen table. Friendships were cemented there; my daughters learned to sew there; and it was where our son's paper route bookkeeping was kept up-to-date.

God's Word gives us some principles to follow as we consider this multifaceted site. His warning is: "For God is not the author of confusion, but of peace..." (1 Corinthians 14:33). This nerve center of our home should set a standard of order. His mandate to us is: "Let all things be done decently and in order" (1 Corinthians 14:40).

Join me as I share some of the projects I do—or have done—at my kitchen table.

Serve Meals

An attractively set table—complete with a tablecloth or pretty place mats, a vase of fresh flowers or greenery, matching dishes set properly, and clean, fresh napkins—projects an invitation to a nutritious, well-planned, and gracious meal.

As my husband, Ben, and I traveled in a conference ministry, we realized that there were very few families who sat down together for a meal. Though it is a brief time, mealtime can be a recharging opportunity for the entire family. Deuteronomy 6:7 states: "And thou shalt teach them [fear or reverential trust of the Lord and the love of the Lord] diligently unto thy children, and shalt talk of them when thou sittest in thine house, and when thou walkest by the way, and when thou liest down, and when thou risest up." I love that it specifies: "When thou sittest in thine house." Yes, at the kitchen table you can fulfill this opportunity to teach these truths to your family.

Because of employment obligations, school activities, or unforeseen delays, there are days when it is impossible to gather the family at mealtime. But don't allow it to become a daily practice. Serving one's self from the refrigerator or cupboard can create a feeling of loneliness and is not the least bit conducive to good nutrition.

We give our families three messages by the way we serve meals. First, we show our attitude toward ourselves: Am I capable of planning and serving nutritious, attractive meals? Second, we project what our attitude is toward them: Are they worth the extra effort it takes to plan and prepare? Third, we show our attitude toward the Lord: Are we joyfully glorifying Him through order and through the encouragement of one another? We find the answer so clearly in God's Word: "Whether therefore ye eat, or drink, or whatsoever ye do, do all to the glory of God" (1 Corinthians 10:31).

Train Your Children to Set the Table

How do you teach children to set the table? Consider making a large place mat from wallpaper, butcher paper, or brown wrapping paper. Using a contrasting paper, draw around, and then cut out, each piece of the place setting: dinner plate, fork, knife, spoon, cup. Glue each piece to the placemat, picturing a proper place setting. Then laminate it or cover both sides with clear Con-Tact® paper to make it durable and easy to clean. Each piece of the place setting is then put over the one pictured on the place mat. This is a wonderful project to do with your child at the kitchen table. How about making a pretty flowered setting for Mom, doll pictures for sister, a favorite vacation-spot place mat for Dad, or a sports theme for big brother?

Have Your Personal Devotions

The kitchen table is a good spot for personal devotions. Romans 12:1–2 states: "I beseech you therefore, brethren, by the mercies of God, that ye present your bodies a living sacrifice, holy, acceptable unto God, which is your reasonable service. And be not conformed to this world: but be ye transformed by the renewing of your mind, that ye may prove what is that good, and acceptable, and perfect, will of God."

My training is in the field of nursing. The first time we went to the hospital ward to give patient care, our assignment was to take the patient's TPR (temperature, pulse, respiration). Upon learning this most basic information about the person, we had some idea of his or her general physical well-being. We can apply the same alliteration to our daily devotions.

***T* is for time.** Set a time to meet the Lord daily. Satan will see to it that you never find the time.

Plan for the time that is right for you—when you are mentally and physically at your best. I have found that the time that works best for me is after breakfast. I am mentally alert at this time of day. The dishes are done, and the general picking up is complete. Then I can sit down and spend uninterrupted time with the Lord.

***P* is for place.** An ideal spot is the kitchen table. Your Bible, notebook, and possibly a concordance or commentary can be fanned out for easy access. Be prepared to write notes on what you have read. Underline Bible passages that are a blessing to you.

***R* is for reading the Word.** Never substitute anything for the Word of God. Use other materials in addition to—but never in place of—your Bible.

You must plan a time, choose a place, and read the Word each day. Your spiritual condition is at stake.

Gather for Family Devotions

The kitchen table is a great place to have family devotions. Often a lady will tell me that she would give anything if her husband would lead in family devotions, but he is not doing it. If this is happening in your home, you may need to have them one-on-one with each child or with your children as a group when your spouse is not present. My husband found that many of the men he talked to sincerely wanted to lead their families in devotions but found themselves intimidated by their wives. Many believed they could not read well enough, especially when reading aloud. They feared mispronouncing words or being unable to interpret the passages, so they simply did not lead in a time of gathering around God's Word as a family.

The time following breakfast is ideal for family devotions. This was the plan we used in our home for several years. When we finished our meal, I picked up my husband's dishes and put them into the sink. In their place in front of him I put a Bible and whatever we were using as a devotional guide at the time. You may wish to share this idea with your husband. Tell him you will be glad to have the Bible and devotional book ready if this is his desire. Never take over his position of spiritual headship. Rather, encourage him and be ready to help him as he desires. He may wish to have various members of the family read each day. This is also a wonderful time to sing together. I recall being with a family who liked to sing one chorus before thanking the Lord for their meal. Even their parakeet joined in with delightful gusto!

What do you do with your Christmas cards when you are done reading them? After removing the cards from the envelopes, transfer the new addresses into your address file, then discard the envelopes. Stack the cards into a pretty basket so that you can take them to your kitchen table. When it is time for family devotions, take the top card from the basket and share any pertinent information about the family who sent the card. Then pray for them that day. You may even drop your friends a note to let them know you prayed for them. I remember how pleased our family was one day in July many years ago. We received just such a note from Ruth Hege, author of *We Two Alone*, telling us that had been the day she had prayed for us. Your family will be reminded of what their friends are doing, and you will have a continued outreach to them through prayer.

To encourage your young children to look forward to family prayer time, make a small photo album (like a "Grandma's Brag Book") in which they have pictures of those for whom they pray regularly. Our friends Bill and Bonnie have done this with their children. The children can turn it from page to page as they pray for parents, sisters and brothers, grandparents, their teachers, their pastor, and missionaries they know. Another idea is to have the children help you make a flip chart of the church missionaries. Whatever method you choose, make the prayer time a vital part of your family devotions.

Keep the length of your family devotions in line with the ages of your children. If you have young children, you probably will not want to exceed ten minutes. Children made to sit through long periods of prayer and Bible reading as a family quickly learn ways of daydreaming to pull down their mental shades. Some will openly rebel against having family devotions, which should be a pleasant, refreshing time.

Create Crafts

Your kitchen table is a convenient place to enjoy crafts. Proverbs 31:27 describes the godly woman: "She looketh well to the ways of her household, and eateth not the bread of idleness." Working on crafts together can be a rewarding way to reach out to an unsaved neighbor or to have fellowship with a new believer. Use this time to share opportunities or blessings that the Lord has given you.

Maybe several of your friends enjoy crafts. This is a great way to get them together.

Teach your children to make interesting projects. Working together on a craft creates a wonderful time to visit with them over the events of the day. Learn what they are thinking about and make this time together refreshing for both of you. I recall a mother telling me she realized that each of her children had a "place" where he or she would visit with her and share things that were important to them. Find your child's "place." It may be the kitchen table.

Our son-in-law Dennis is a skilled craftsman in his free time. He cut out wooden pieces for necklaces, then our daughter Karen and their children, Joshua and Jillian, painted them at the kitchen table. We all still treasure some of their innovative crafts.

Create a useful craft to take to shut-ins or to friends in a nursing home. They will feel like it's a ray of sunshine. Create a large fabric "pocket" that could drape over the arm of a chair to hold their Bible, books, or papers. Or make a pretty cloth-covered box for storing some of their treasures. A lady would love a silk flower arrangement or pillow corsage. You could make each of these at your kitchen table.

Fashion your own basket to hold Christmas cards from your friends. Spray paint it to match your room. Add a pretty bow and streamer trailing down the side of the handle. Or stencil your basket, rubber stamp it, or weave a ribbon into the reed of the basket. Be creative! Crafts do not need to be expensive; they should simply be an expression of your talents and careful planning.

On one trip to a mission field, I purchased a scarf for each of the missionary ladies and teenage girls. I planned to have a session with them to teach different ways to tie scarves so that they would get plenty of use from them. Our daughter Brenda made earrings to match each of the scarves. It made a charming set, and the ladies were delighted to choose the set that suited their colors and clothing. Of course, this project took place at our kitchen table. When we arrived in Africa, it was at the missionaries' kitchen tables that they made their choices.

If you learn a new craft, share the joy and blessing with someone else—at your kitchen table.

Teach a Younger Lady

The kitchen table is a wonderful place for older ladies to teach younger ladies to sew, cook, bake, mend, or do a myriad of other household skills. Younger women long to know how to teach their children character qualities, how to respond to their husbands, or how to find time to keep themselves and their homes attractive. In Titus

2:3–5 we are admonished: "The aged women likewise, that they be in behaviour as becometh holiness, not false accusers, not given to much wine, teachers of good things; That they may teach the young women to be sober, to love their husbands, to love their children, To be discreet, chaste, keepers at home, good, obedient to their own husbands, that the Word of God be not blasphemed."

I can recall when I thought this passage from Titus was referring only to old ladies. Have you considered that each of us is older than someone? When our children were young, they thought the teenagers were the "old ladies" and often considered them to be their models, mimicking everything the teens did.

I have taught several young ladies to make sourdough bread at our kitchen table. Often a young wife would ask me to teach her how to bake bread. It was a delight to see her learn how to knead the dough (sometimes having it clear up to her elbows!). Then she discovered that when she pulled forward with her fingers, then pushed away with the palm of her hand, it was not a messy job at all. After she kneaded the bread, we sat at the table and had some wonderful talks about the important concerns of life, home, family, and God's Word.

Lead Someone to Christ

The kitchen table is a wonderful place to lead someone to Christ! Acts 1:8 says, "But ye shall receive power, after that the Holy Ghost is come upon you: and ye shall be witnesses unto me both in Jerusalem, and in all Judaea, and in Samaria, and unto the uttermost part of the earth." Right there at the kitchen table can be your "Jerusalem." God's Word is clear in showing us that all have sinned. There is nothing we can do to save ourselves. Christ came to take our sin upon Himself and die in our place. Repenting, then realizing we must personally accept what Christ has done in our stead, by grace through faith, we accept that free gift of salvation. (On page 96, you can read more about how to accept—and share—this gift.)

Help a New Christian to Grow

The kitchen table is an ideal place to help a new Christian grow in her faith. There are many books you may use, such as *Won by One,* by Mel Lacock, which may be used over a period of several weeks. This book is designed in such a way that both of you prepare at home, then go over the material together. You can often get people to join you for a Bible study who would not visit your church. Take advantage of these opportunities that are all around you.

Show Hospitality

Have a home that is open to guests. Your kitchen table should be a place where there are opportunities for fellowship and spiritual refreshment. Hebrews 13:1–2 states: "Let brotherly love continue. Be not forgetful to entertain strangers: for thereby some have entertained angels unawares."

Many families are not comfortable having guests in their home. The reasons they use are, first, that they are too busy, and second, that it costs too much. Scripture does not seem to make those exceptions. Remember, we give the most to whatever is most important to us. Scripture clearly tells us to have guests in our home. Demonstrating hospitality will teach your children to think of others, to be friendly, and to share what God has given to them. We can have a rich ministry to others by making them welcome in our home.

As we traveled in our family conference ministry, it was a blessing when people had us in their homes for meals or snacks. The fellowship and the warmth of Christian love encouraged our hearts. It also helped us to get acquainted with families. Many times at church we did not see the entire family together. In their home we saw them in their own setting and had a fresh perspective on them as a family unit. What a joy that was to us!

Your material possessions are not what your guests will remember, but rather, they will remember what you are willing to share. In your home and at your kitchen table, you share yourself.

What you serve need not be expensive or difficult to prepare. In this day when people are very conscious of not eating foods high in fats, do not feel that you must bake pies or cakes. Serve a bowl of fresh fruit or have it attractively cut and laid out on a pretty plate. You may wish to have cheese and crackers with it. It is ideal if you have some ready-made dry mixes so that spontaneous invitations are possible. Allow your guests to help prepare the table and the food, providing a great opportunity for you to visit with them. Ingredients for do-it-yourself sandwiches also make a nice snack, allowing the guests to add only what they enjoy.

One lady shared with me that on Sunday evening before leaving for church, she would put a double batch of onion soup into the crock pot. She had toasted, thinly sliced bagel rounds ready. Her family always invited someone home with them for a light treat afterward. It smelled wonderful when they walked into the house, and all the preparation was done. The kitchen table became a place for warm fellowship with new friends.

Beverages can vary with the likes and dislikes of your own family and friends. You don't need to purchase expensive beverages. Apple cider in season is a treat. Coffee, hot or iced tea, milk, or just a cold glass of water is always pleasant. Especially if there are young children present, do not serve sweet or colored beverages. Most young mothers say it takes the fun out of the fellowship, because they are worrying about the children spilling the beverage, and they may have visions of staying up all night with a hyperactive child. Either milk or water is ideal for a youngster.

Write Letters

Proverbs 25:25 says, "As cold waters to a thirsty soul, so is good news from a far country." Letter writing is the last item on too many of our "must-do" lists. What a blessing it is to get a letter from a friend. A thank-you note for something you have done or a note of encouragement when you need it can be that "cold water to a thirsty soul."

When we were in Mali and Niger with some of our missionaries, they said, "Please take our picture reading this letter." One of the missionaries had received a personal letter and was sharing it with everyone. Our missionaries go to an empty mailbox too frequently. How often has a missionary your church supports come home after several years on another continent and felt like a total stranger? Why? Because no one took the time to write and let him or her know what was going on. Nobody followed the needs and joys that missionary family had on their field of ministry. From our kitchen tables, we can reach around the world. Are we doing that?

Pretty note paper can be very costly. This causes some to think that it is a luxury to write letters to people they do not know well. Use an interesting rubber stamp design on plain paper, then write your note in that same color of ink. Stencil some charming designs. Embossing makes elegant notes for special messages. Go to a craft shop in your area and learn how to do these things. Even better, do this with a friend. Do you have a fountain pen? The quiet whisper of that pen gliding over the paper on your kitchen table is calming and refreshing.

When someone has done something for you, take a few minutes to write him or her a thank-you note. You do not need to mail it through the postal system if it is someone you see regularly.

Tuck a note of thanks inside the cover of your friend's Bible or notebook and tell him or her that you are being a private "mail carrier." The recipient will love it.

Following your bridal shower, wedding, or baby shower, get those thank-you notes off right away. People have given time and money to purchase gifts for you. It is only gracious on your part to respond with appreciation. I hear many people say that they have not yet received any thanks for large gifts they gave several months ago.

Have you written a note of thanks to an older person lately? Let this individual know what his or her consistent testimony has meant to you and your family. Before my husband passed away in 2015, he received letters of gratitude and cards filled with treasured memories from friends. We read these aloud multiple times, and our hearts were encouraged with every reading. It brought us great joy to know that he heard these things while he was still living rather than for us to simply hear *about* them after he was gone. Pastors need to receive notes of appreciation for faithfulness in preaching the Word of God. A young child who has prepared an instrumental or vocal solo for a church service needs your encouragement. Maybe it was not done with all the finesse of a professional musician, or maybe he or she was shaking with fear. Knowing that someone appreciated it will give this child more confidence next time. Keep your note paper near your kitchen table so that you can be an encourager.

Prepare Albums and Treasures

If you are a grandmother, have you written informative comments, names, and dates on the backs of your pictures? If you are a young person, maybe you need to sit down at the kitchen table with your grandmother. While she tells you the history of the photos, you can be the secretary.

My mother often told me about old photographs of events where there were cousins I had never met. I knew she would tell me about them again many times. "Someday I will write that down." My mother is now with the Lord, and I do not remember the dates, events, or names of many of those in her pictures. I say this to my shame.

If you are not going to get your pictures into a photo album, you may just want to put them into a shoe box. Put dividers by years, by family, or by event—whatever best fits your need. Write on the back who is in the picture, then when you can put them into the album, they are ready.

A few years ago, when our family was together for Christmas, I pulled out a basket of unfiled pictures I had accumulated. We all sat around the kitchen table. Each one chose pictures about which he or she knew something special. They each dated the pictures approximately and made some notation about the event on the back of each one. It was such a refreshing time of recalling the growing years of our family. My plan had been that we would work on it for about half an hour. An hour and a half later we stopped. It was a wonderful way of sharing childhood experiences with our daughters' spouses, who did not know our family during those years. I also ended up with a good-sized box of pictures ready for an album!

Do you have recipes that were handed down from your ethnic background? My mother's side of the family is Norwegian. That means that I have the family recipes for lefsa and, of course, lutefisk. My dad is of English descent, so my pasty recipe is well-used. Sit down at the kitchen table with one of the older generation of your family and get those recipes in writing. Many families long for something "like Grandma used to make," and nobody knows how to make it. Of course, the recipes may be explained by "handfuls" or "pinches," so be prepared to do some conversions to cups and teaspoons.

Prepare for Teaching

Your kitchen table is a great place to prepare your Sunday school Lesson. Colossians 3:23 states: "And whatsoever ye do, do it heartily, as to the Lord, and not unto men." Don't simply prepare your Sunday school lesson on Saturday night. Begin the Sunday afternoon *before* you will be teaching the lesson. That will give you ample time to add fresh illustrations and look for appropriate pictures or object lessons to make your teaching come alive! We need to prepare with the determination that our class has been entrusted to us, and that we will give an account for how we have taught them. Scripture admonishes them to respond to that teaching, but our concern is to present the lesson in a clear and understandable way.

Enjoy After-School Snacks

Your kitchen table is a fantastic place to have time with your children right after they get home from school. If it is a cold day, have some hot chocolate ready. If it has been hot, fix some lemonade or iced tea. You will regret it if you think that you are too busy. Those years are too quickly gone. Savor every possible moment of sharing. Sit down with them and enjoy the refreshment, even if it is only for a few minutes. It is time invested that will bring many treasured memories later. They will quickly share the events of their school day before the busyness of evening chores, jobs, or homework begins.

A dear friend gave us a lovely tea set when our children were young. During the years Marcia and Karen were in high school and Brenda was in elementary school, I would have something in the teapot for us to share after school. It may have only been for a few moments, but they were refreshing times that brought a sense of security in being home together. Many mothers today are working outside the home. If at all possible, arrange to be home when your children first arrive from school so that you can enjoy those moments with them around your kitchen table.

Help with Homework

Children often do their homework at the kitchen table. You can help your children with their homework, but mothers, be careful not to ever do it *for* them. Some of the saddest stories I have heard in counseling relate to heartbreaking failures in life that go back to a parent doing a child's homework. Too many children grow up thinking that if they do not get the job done, someone else will do it for them.

I recall my friend Sarah telling me about a party she attended one evening. The mother of a first grader excused herself early, saying that she had some things to do at home. Then she whispered to Sarah as she was leaving, "I have to go home and do Ryan's homework. We can't let him fail first grade."

Sarah told her friend that she may be wise to let Ryan fail now instead of later. However, it fell on deaf ears. How often our selfish pride cannot handle the failure of one of our children—not because of what it would do to the child, but because of what we think it would do to the family reputation. If your child does not comprehend the material on his or her present grade level, why would you ever think of pushing him or her to get to the next level, only to be far more confused? This becomes a deepening rut from which much harm can come to the child.

I read that Albert Einstein was seven before he could read; Winston Churchill failed the sixth grade; and Thomas Edison was told by his teachers that he was too stupid to learn anything. Because the neighbor's child is reading at age five does not mean that your child will read at age five. Nor, because your child can work complicated math problems at nine, should you expect this of other children. We must encourage and help our children to have a thirst for knowledge and an excitement in finding it for themselves.

Plan Your Day

Your kitchen table is the perfect place to make your list for the day. An ideal time to do that is right after having your devotions. Devotions are the first thing on your list, and you can already put a checkmark after that! If you do not set goals for your day, how will you know when you have arrived at a worthwhile conclusion? One lady shared with me that her husband would sometimes note something that needed attention around the house. He would do it, and then he would add it to her list and put a checkmark after it!

Plan to make one contact for the Lord each day. It may be by writing a letter to someone who is grieving, making a phone call to a shut-in, or offering a word of encouragement to a discouraged friend. It may be through a visit to an unsaved neighbor to share something you baked and then to share the gift of salvation.

Include on your list every day something that you dread doing. Maybe for you it is sewing on buttons or patching those jeans for the fourth time. Could it be cleaning the oven? (I am still trusting that someday someone will invent one that flushes!) Then include something you do not feel worthy to take the time to do. This may be manicuring your nails, arranging a pretty bouquet of flowers, reading an extra chapter in a book that you would like to finish, or trying a new hairstyle. If at all possible, plan to read one chapter of a book every day. Be realistic in your planning. If you make no plan, the urgent things will probably take priority over the important things. Then you will wonder how the day slipped away. Do not tie yourself to your list, however. The Lord may have better plans for your day.

Make Treasured Family Heirlooms

The kitchen table is a wonderful place to prepare unique gifts. Grandparents, record yourself as you read a book to your grandchild. You can also record a bedtime story, tell the child that you love him or her, and say "good-night."

Our daughter Brenda had my dad, her grandpa, spend a week with her. While he was there, they sat down at the kitchen table, where Dad made a birthday gift for me. My dad was eighty-seven years old at the time, was an amputee, was almost blind, and was quite hard of hearing. But he carefully planned what he wanted to tell me.

With the recorder on the table, he shared memories of taking me to the one-room country school, using the team of horses and wagon or sleigh. He told how at Christmastime, he would put bells on the horses. There was straw in the box of the sleigh, and there was a horsehide robe as a warm cover for us. He had a horsehide coat and big mittens to match the robe. He recalled for me how he would call out, "It's time for school," as we approached the homes of the other children who lived between our home and school. The children would come out and climb into the sleigh, and off we would go to the next home.

Dad also told of going rag-a-muffin when he was a young boy. The family would pile into the sleigh, each one in a costume to conceal his or her identity. They would go to a neighbor's home and see if that family could guess who was in the group. Then that family was added to the merry ride through the country. It usually included singing and refreshments.

He recalled threshing and all the work Mother would do to feed twenty or more men. The neighbor ladies came too, and everyone made an event of threshing time. It made me recall that I would sit out on the steps beside the house and peel potatoes. Somehow, more than the work of peeling the potatoes, I remembered that there were some little blue flowers that grew in the cracks of the cement. They looked so winsome and seemed to lighten what otherwise may have been a wearisome task. The chatter of the ladies and the smell of roasting meat and fresh pies filled the air.

Little did I know, when I listened to that tape, that my Dad would be with the Lord before my next birthday. The time he and Brenda spent at the kitchen table continues to bring warmth and joy. I have since made a copy of that recording for each of our children.

Prepare for Future Hunger Attacks

Prepare your family's favorite cookie dough. Roll it into logs and freeze them in plastic bags. When the children need a special treat, allow them to get a bag of the dough from the freezer, slice it on the cutting board at the kitchen table, and bake. Then comes the wonderful aroma of fresh-baked cookies! Wait for the giggles of delight as they devour them with glasses of cold milk.

Play Table Games

The kitchen table is the ideal spot for playing table games. Scrabble®, checkers, Pictionary®, and other family favorites can be great fun. When our children get together, they always plan a game of Monopoly. Sometimes it goes well into the night, even to the point of forming corporations to topple our son-in-law Brent, the Monopoly expert of the family.

Share Family Fun

How long since your family has become an orchestra—"a comb band," that is? A comb with a piece of waxed paper wrapped around it makes a delightful sound when it is properly blown. Of course, there will be some tingling lips in the process, but it will be worth it. After a meal, it would be such fun to have the combs and waxed paper ready for your family to enjoy. Age is no barrier to this grand orchestra.

International news often reveals names of countries that we adults are embarrassed to admit we did not know existed. You may want to have a large world map near your kitchen table. School-age children can point out places referred to in the news, and everyone will learn together.

Make Collections

Learning about favorite collections, compiling them, and cleaning or framing them is great fun at the kitchen table. When our son, Ed, was in junior high school, he had a paper route. He found many interesting coins after he collected the weekly fees from his route. This was often followed by time at the kitchen table, sorting and getting the collectable coins into their proper folders.

Our children cut out cartoons (like Family Circus©) from the daily newspaper. Then on a rainy day, they would go to the kitchen table, trim the edges neatly, and glue them into spiral notebooks. These "homemade comic books" made great gifts for friends and missionaries.

Read Together

Does your family have a reading time? I recall a lady in my Sunday school class who grew up hearing her dad read Shakespeare every evening. When she went to kindergarten, she thought everyone came from a reading family like hers. She was so disappointed to learn that the other children didn't even know who Romeo and Juliet were. Right after the evening meal may be a cozy time for your family to share a daily chapter from a book.

If your reading time is limited, you may want to do it at the kitchen table so that you can enjoy your favorite cup filled with that special blend of tea. Make sure that the books you read align with this portrait from Scripture: "Finally, brethren, whatsoever things are true, whatsoever things are honest, whatsoever things are just, whatsoever things are pure, whatsoever things are lovely, whatsoever things are of good report; if there be any virtue, and if there be any praise, think on these things" (Philippians 4:8).

Encourage an Impaired Child

The mother of a mentally handicapped child shared that she and her son would often share time at the kitchen table. Barbara said that each time there was a highlight in Peter's life, they would glue a sticker, picture, paper, or special treasure into a notebook. Peter had that notebook to show his friends the events of importance to him.

Disperse Allowance

You can give your children their allowance while at the kitchen table. When they are young, give the money in small coins. Teach them early that the first portion belongs to the Lord; the second goes into savings for a later time; the rest may be used for wants and needs. Establish this pattern early in life. Our children began getting an allowance when they were three years old. We believed it prepared each one for the financial realities of life. It gave them the confidence of knowing what they had to share, save, and spend. This had ripple effects into every area of their lives. I especially recall trips to the store for grocery shopping. They were actually pleasant times, because the children rarely made pleas for special treats. They knew that if they had the money, they could purchase them. If they did not, it was fruitless to ask.

Teach Etiquette

Some families like to have Manners Night around the table. This is the night when everyone dresses in Sunday-best clothes and pays extra attention to being gracious. It is a wonderful time to teach a new rule of etiquette.

Teach your children early that unless there is an emergency, they do not leave the table until everyone is finished. When the meal is over, each child must give one compliment about something he or she liked, thank the preparer for the meal, then ask to be excused. They are going to learn this best as they see and hear the adults doing it. The etiquette book is only a supplement to that teaching.

Create Family Memories

Holidays are treasured times when the family gets together. I often enjoyed making two double batches of gingerbread men before the family came for Christmas. I did not decorate them, but I had a supply of raisins and various colors of icing ready. My plan the first year was that our four grandchildren—Joshua, Jillian, Janelle, and Eric—would have fun decorating them. However, the adult members of the family began appearing one by one and had as much fun as the children. It was amazing how much we learned about each one's past year as those little gingerbread men were creatively decorated.

Ben and I prepared a table gift for each member of the family when we had our Christmas Eve meal. It recalled something about that person's year since we were last together. It may have revealed something that he or she had not planned to reveal—like a traffic ticket, which may have shown up via a gift in the form of a miniature traffic officer. These were always light and humorous types of gifts and never anything expensive. They provided a fun time for sharing as a family.

Display Gifts from Your Children

When your children bring you a present, whether from the backyard, from school, or from Sunday school, place it where everyone can enjoy it. If it is flowers from the yard, you can tell the age of the gift giver by the length of the flower stems. The little toddler pulls the flower from where it is attached to the stem. These float beautifully in a shallow bowl. As your children grow, these are followed by blossoms with stems that are long enough to be place in a container the size of a water glass. Then come the longer stems that go into one of your favorite vases. Children love knowing that what they brought you was to your liking, and that you wanted to display it for everyone to see. What better place could there be than the center of your kitchen table?

Conclusion

Luke 2:52 tells us, "And Jesus increased in wisdom and stature, and in favour with God and man." We have seen how much we can do right there at our kitchen tables. It can be a place where wisdom is applied (mental growth); stature is increased (physical growth); favor with God is deepened (spiritual growth); and favor with man is practiced (social growth). Our families must grow in the same areas in which our Lord Jesus Christ grew. Teaching through conversation, observation, and imitation is as natural as breathing when it happens at the kitchen table.

From my kitchen to yours, thank you for sitting down with me so I could share a few of the things I do right here. I hope you will utilize every possible opportunity at your kitchen table. Let your family and friends know how special they are to you—and to the Lord. There is no better spot to do this than at your kitchen table.

BIBLICAL SELF IMAGE

If I were to put my tape measure around your middle, how big would it show your waistline to be? I'll let you in on a secret: because my measuring tape is elastic, I could make you any size you wanted to be! All too often when we look at ourselves, we use an "elastic" standard of measurement. We look at someone else and think, "Why can't I look like that?" But we cannot measure ourselves by anyone else and have the results be accurate. We can never be exactly like anyone else. That is not God's plan. We are each one of a kind!

Second Corinthians 10:12 states, "For we dare not make ourselves of the number, or compare ourselves with some that commend themselves: but they measuring themselves by themselves, and comparing themselves among themselves, are not wise." As we compare ourselves with others, we will never measure up to what they are. They will never measure up to what *we* are. No two people are alike. (If they were, one of them would be unnecessary!)

The only standard by which we can accurately measure our lives is the Word of God. We need to be in God's Word daily to develop a self-image measured by God's unchanging standard. In Psalm 139:13–16 we read: "For thou hast possessed my reins: thou hast covered me in my mother's womb. I will praise thee; for I am fearfully and wonderfully made: marvelous are thy works; and that my soul knoweth right well. My substance was not hid from thee, when I was made in secret, and curiously wrought in the lowest parts of the earth. Thine eyes did see my substance, yet being unperfect; and in thy book all my members were written, which in continuance were fashioned, when as yet there was none of them." God has a plan for your life. You were fashioned to carry out that plan.

If you feel your nose is too long (you are too skinny, too tall, too short, your skin coloring is not what you would have chosen, your feet are too large, etc.), just ask God, "What do you want me to show through what I think is my imperfection?" That may be the door to your mission field. As you go into a shoe store and ask to order size 13 shoes, it could be an opportunity to show a sweet attitude about the way God has made you and to share a testimony to the Lord's all-knowing goodness. You may be a witness to someone who has not heard a Christian testimony before.

Ephesians 2:10 states, "For we are his workmanship, created in Christ Jesus unto good works, which God hath before ordained that we should walk in them." Do we believe we are God's workmanship? When we put ourselves down, we are telling a holy God that He has made a mistake. Would we knowingly accuse God of such an error? We need to see ourselves clearly in the light of God's Word.

Philippians 1:6 states: "Being confident of this very thing, that he which hath begun a good work in you will perform it until the day of Jesus Christ." Whatever you might think is your imperfection, remember that God wants to use it in His plan for you—"until the day of Jesus Christ."

Your Inner Self

Is there at least one person who cares what happens to you? Have you ever awakened to what seemed like a cold, uncaring world and thought, "Nobody cares what happens to me. I could have been dead for six weeks, and nobody would have missed me"? If you know Christ as your Savior, you have Someone who cares deeply about what happens to you! Romans 5:8 says, "But God commendeth His love toward us, in that, while we were yet sinners, Christ died for us." God did not wait for us to become beautiful and then decide whether or not He would love us. God loved us while we were sinners and sent His Only Son, the Lord Jesus Christ, to die in our place so that we could spend an eternity in heaven with a holy God. This is how much my God loves you—and me. Don't ever feel that nobody loves you or that nobody cares. God does! Since Christ died in your place, you obviously have value in His sight.

Keep attractive on the inside. In Galatians 2:20 we are told, "I am crucified with Christ: nevertheless I live; yet not I, but Christ liveth in me: and the life which I now live in the flesh I live by the faith of the Son of God, who loved me, and gave himself for me." This dependence is a picture of humility.

Humility is knowing yourself, accepting yourself, and then being yourself.

We are to be channels through which Christ is seen and magnified. The greatest barrier to that channel is pride. Pride is denial—through self-love—of Divine authority. Proverbs 3:5–6 teaches us: "Trust in the Lord with all thine heart; and lean not unto thine own understanding. In all thy ways acknowledge Him, and He shall direct thy paths."

Spend time in God's Word. Your daily devotions should be the highlight of your day. Don't let them become a meaningless ritual. (See pages 62–66 for my personal method.)

Read good books about people who have been used of God. What is placed in the well of our hearts will come up in the bucket of our thoughts, actions, and words. By this, I mean that our minds are much like an old country well, where there was a bucket on a rope. The bucket was released from its "hold position" and lowered into the water. When it was wound up by the rope, whatever was in that well came up in the bucket. What we read affects who we are. Proverbs 23:7 says, "For as he thinketh in his heart, so is he...." As I stated in the previous chapter, Philippians 4:8 gives us a great checklist for filling our minds: "Finally, brethren, whatsoever things are true, whatsoever things are honest, whatsoever things are just, whatsoever things are pure, whatsoever things are lovely, whatsoever things are of good report; if there be any virtue, and if there be any praise, think on these things." Your mind will be more inclined to think on godly things if you are reading that which is godly.

Associate with people who strengthen your walk. Psalm 1:1 demonstrates this for us: "Blessed is the man that walketh not in the counsel of the ungodly, nor standeth in the way of sinners, nor sitteth in the seat of the scornful." We are often known by our choice of friends. We naturally gravitate to those who think as we think. Associate with people who will build you up and with those you will build up in return. Proverbs 27:17 informs us: "Iron sharpeneth iron; so a man sharpeneth the countenance of his friend." A godly friend can confront us when we are faltering or can encourage us when we are weak.

Make a list of your positive qualities and thank God for them. It is such human nature to be conscious of every fault we have and to ask God, "Why?" But at the same time, we take the many gifts God has graciously given us for granted. God made us. He wants us to use what He has given us for His glory. First Corinthians 6:19–20 directs us with these words: "What? know ye not that your body is the temple of the Holy Spirit which is in you, which ye have of God, and ye are not your own? For ye are bought with a price: therefore glorify God in your body, and in your spirit, which are God's."

Have you ever complained about not getting your hair to lay the way you wanted it to, then you went to the store and met your friend who had just completed her chemotherapy? She had no hair. Such a simple thing as having hair is a blessing! I recall grumbling about the poor circulation in my legs until my dear dad had a leg amputated. How thankful I am for two legs.

Let's say we have our arm in a cast for several weeks. We will look forward to having the cast removed. We eagerly anticipate being able to move our arm freely once again. However, when the doctor removes the cast, we feel disappointment, because the arm has atrophied (meaning that it is smaller and weaker than before). In the medical profession, we would call this "atrophy of disuse": because it has not been used, it is not useable. Many of our God-given gifts and talents have atrophied because they have not been used. We must use the talents God has given to us!

Avoid negative input. I recall hearing a lady say that she loved getting the morning paper so she could check her horoscope. During the day when something unusual happened, her thoughts naturally focused on what her horoscope had said. Stay away from filling your mind with such information! When the unexpected happens during your day, your time in God's Word will prompt you to recall, dwell on, and claim His promises!

Pornography, soap operas, gossip columns, and other ploys of the world for our minds can also be considered negative input. They do not support the standards we have set for ourselves or our families. Neither do they meet the standard set forth in Psalm 101:3: "I will set no wicked thing before mine eyes."

As a parent, be sure not to use put-downs when disciplining your children (such as telling your child that he or she will never be liked because he is so fat or because she is such a slouch). Instead, help him to correct his eating habits or help her to change her slovenly attitude. Remember, you are dealing with the problem, not the person. Many adults say that they were told as a child that they had no talents, were ugly, were dumb, or were in some way incapable. These things are difficult to forget. They come back to mind when a task is overwhelming or when there is discouragement. Because of their feelings of inferiority, many find themselves thinking that they can never meet the challenges they face.

Learn from successful failures. Thomas Edison tried ten thousand times before inventing the light bulb. When he succeeded, a

Detroit newspaper reporter interviewed him and asked how it felt to have failed ten thousand times before finally having his invention in working order. Mr. Edison told the reporter that he had never failed but had learned ten thousand ways it could not be done. Many times that statement has encouraged me. I tend to get to the end of some days and look back at how many attempted tasks ended in failure. Now I can look back and realize that I learned a few more ways those tasks could not be done. It is much more encouraging, and the outlook is far brighter!

A gentleman in our church in Indiana was a paraplegic because of a horse-riding accident. He easily could have taken to his wheelchair and lived on the sympathy of all of us. Instead, he strengthened his upper-body muscles through exhausting exercise and tireless effort. He went places in his wheelchair that most of us with strong bodies would not have walked. He was an encourager to the men who worked for him. Our family will never forget the Fourth of July when he called us on his car phone to ask if we liked blueberries. He had been to the patch (in his wheelchair) to pick us a bucket of fresh blueberries. Believe me, we savored every berry! We felt honored to have had Mr. Brown in our church family and as a friend.

Work on those areas in your life that are distracting from your biblical self-image. If you are having a problem with crudeness in etiquette, get an etiquette book. Crude, tactless qualities have no place in the life of a Christian. How many Christians are thankless? Take time to show appreciation. Have you written a note of thanks to a young person who played his or her instrument in your church recently? Have you thanked your pastor for his faithfulness in preaching the Word of God? Have you thanked your parents for their encouragement to you and for their provision for you as a child?

For starters, determine that by Tuesday of each week, you will write one note or letter of encouragement. Plan that by Thursday of each week you will have made a phone call to someone who is hurting. Ask the Lord to lay on your heart those who need your supporting words and actions.

Maybe tidiness is a problem for you. Many young ladies have shared with me that they have not had a role model to prepare them for tidiness and housework. For a variety of reasons, their mothers had neither the time nor the desire to make their home a pleasant place, so they are at a loss to know where to begin. There are many good books on making housework efficient and enjoyable. *The Messies Superguide,* by Sandra Felton, is a helpful and refreshing book!

Do you have a lack of compassion? Jude 22 says, "And of some have compassion, making a difference." Compassion causes us to look outside of ourselves to the needs of those around us. Often within our family of believers, needs go unnoticed, and this shows unbelievers our lack of compassion. Why should they want our Savior if we are so consumed with self that we have no time to feel the hurts of others in God's family or to attempt to meet their needs?

Unbecoming habits of the past can be changed. With God's help, those old habits can be replaced with biblical new habits. Second Corinthians 5:17 instructs us: "Therefore if any man be in Christ, he is a new creature: old things are passed away; behold, all things are become new." *How to Say No to a Stubborn Habit,* by Erwin Lutzer, is a great book on this topic. Don't allow an area over which you can exercise discipline to scar an otherwise godly life.

Your Outer Self

Keep attractive on the outside. General appearance, whether it is our clothing selection, color choices, conduct, or countenance, should show what is in the heart. In fact, we give three messages through our appearance: our attitude toward ourselves, our attitude toward others, and our attitude toward the Lord. First Samuel 16:7 states: "The Lord seeth not as man seeth; for man looketh on the outward appearance, but the Lord looketh on the heart." It is easy for us to say that the outside appearance does not matter, because God looks on the heart. Yet we must realize that this verse also clearly tells us that because people cannot look on the heart, they look to the outside appearance, which *reveals* what is in the heart.

Many Christians are cautious about high fashion and trendy appearance in their clothing. Have you ever thought that wearing clothing that is twenty years out of style is just as much—if not more—of a plea to be noticed? In a day when thrift stores are plentiful and tag sales are available, there is little excuse to look dowdy, even for those on a meager income. Looking "frumpy" is not honoring to our Lord, who admonishes us in 1 Corinthians 10:31: "Whether therefore ye eat, or drink, or whatsoever ye do, do all to the glory of God."

First Timothy 2:9–10 is explicit about modesty in dress: "In like manner also, that women adorn themselves in modest apparel, with shamefacedness and sobriety; not with braided hair, or gold, or pearls, or costly array; but which becometh women professing godliness with good works." Dress in such a way that the first part of your body to be noticed is your face. I enjoy wearing scarves tied in various fascinating ways. I find that they not only keep the attention near my face, but they are wonderful wardrobe stretchers, and I can pack them easily for travel. There are a number of books in your local library or bookstore to help with color and fabric selection and to help you find styles that are becoming to your height, weight, and build.

Set short-term goals on the way to reaching your long-term goals. If you feel that you are unpleasingly pudgy and think you need to lose fifty pounds, that is a worthwhile goal. By when do you wish to have lost those fifty pounds? How much per week do you feel confident that you can lose (with a doctor-assisted or approved plan)? Let us assume that you can wisely lose one and one-half pounds per week. By the end of the first month, you will have lost six pounds. In eight and one-third months, you could reach your goal. Make sure you allow for plateaus—during which you cannot seem to lose an ounce—and plan for ten months. Don't let those times change your course. When you reach your goal, you will feel that you have won a great victory! If you do not set those short-term goals, you will be discouraged, because you have not lost the entire amount right away. However, do not use fad diets; you will more than likely gain back more than you lost!

You can even apply the principle of short-term and long-term goals to your housekeeping. You can set a long-term goal as to when you want the house to have had its thorough cleaning, painting, or maybe even some updating. However, you must first set short-term goals. By the end of month one, strive to have certain rooms completed. By the end of month two, the next set of rooms should be done. This way you will keep the goal in focus. It will help you realize that this is a long process that is going to require discipline.

Meeting your short-term goals gives you a feeling of accomplishment and of being on track. Proverbs 13:19 tells us, "The desire accomplished is sweet to the soul...."

Never compare yourself with someone else. Remember that 2 Corinthians 10:12 states: "For we dare not make ourselves of the number, or compare ourselves with some that commend themselves: but they measuring themselves by themselves, and comparing themselves among themselves, are not wise." No two people have the same talents or areas of ministry. We are unique in our abilities to reach others and serve the Lord.

In John 21:22, Jesus is speaking to Peter and says, "If I will that he tarry till I come, what is that to thee? follow thou me." Peter had been looking at John, and Jesus had to remind him that he was not accountable for John but for himself. I, too, will have to give an account for what I have done with the talents God has given me, not those given to someone else.

I grew up on a farm. My Dad took painstaking care of his horses, but he expected them to do a day's work and to do it well. Old Barney, his sorrel horse, had a stubborn will sometimes. Instead of looking ahead at the row they were plowing, he would look at the other horse on the team, and the result would be a crooked furrow. Dad would have to put blinders on Barney so that he could only look straight ahead. Then the furrows were straight.

When we focus on our own task and do it to please our Lord, the resulting accomplishment will be far superior. Colossians 3:23–24 states: "And whatsoever ye do, do it heartily, as to the Lord, and not unto men; knowing that of the Lord ye shall receive the reward of the inheritance: for ye serve the Lord Christ."

Learn to smile often. Have you ever known someone who rarely smiled? Didn't you feel burdened for that person, wondering what was causing the heaviness of his or her heart? Proverbs 15:13 tells us, "A merry heart maketh a cheerful countenance...." Proverbs 17:22 says, "A merry heart doeth good like a medicine: but a broken spirit drieth the bones." If it is not easy for you to smile, practice smiling in front of a mirror. Your witness for Christ will be greatly enhanced as your countenance reflects the joy of the Lord.

A young lady sent me a list of eight things that a winning smile will help us do: gain friends, get a job (nobody wants a grumpy employee around the shop), keep a happier home, impress our teacher, influence our boss, stimulate our colleagues, excite our lover, and finally, inspire our self-confidence. Work on smiling if you need to—not for your glory, but for God's glory.

Be a blessing to those you come in contact with. Matthew 20:28 shows us Christ's view of ministry for Himself. "Even as the Son of man came not to be ministered unto, but to minister, and to give his life a ransom for many." We must be an open channel, willing to allow the Holy Spirit to work through us to encourage and minister to other people. If you find there is a time when you are discouraged or when your focus is on yourself instead of on the Lord and others, find someone with a need and meet that need. Your own problem will fade in comparison.

Look people in the eye when you are talking to them. Did you ever talk to someone who could not look into your eyes? You assumed he or she wanted to ask you a question, but that individual stood looking at the floor instead of looking at you. Did you get the feeling he or she would rather be doing something else or that he or she wasn't telling you the truth? We think of the eyes as the window to the soul. When you are speaking to your child, do you insist that he or she looks into your eyes? Gently place both hands under the chin of your little one and ask him or her to look at your eyes while you are speaking. You will only have to give the instruction once. You are doing yourself and your child a wonderful favor. Many employers believe that the person who will not look into the interviewer's eyes cannot be trusted.

Use your time wisely. Matthew 6:33, my life verse, states: "But seek ye first the kingdom of God, and His righteousness; and all these things shall be added unto you." You will give the most time to that which is most important to you. Be sure that the Lord has first place in your day, and He will guide you. Many times a day I use

Matthew 6:33 as my standard of measurement when I need to make choices about the use of my time.

I was preparing to speak at a ladies' retreat about eight hours from our home and had a number of the usual last-minute details that needed my attention. One of them was to have Judy, a lady in our church who graciously kept my hair cut and permed, trim and set my hair. I compiled my morning list, including going to Judy's house (this would take an hour and a half), having my personal devotions, and accomplishing various other tasks. In reviewing my list, I found that I needed more time than what I had available. I rationalized that I could have my devotions on the trip, but I had to do everything else before leaving. Soon the Lord convicted me through Matthew 6:33 that I was going in reverse in my decision making. The "must-do" was my time with the Lord in His Word. Just as I finished my Bible reading and prayer time, the phone rang. It was Judy: "Lorraine, I am sorry, but I am going to have to go out of town. Could I stop by your house, instead of your coming over here, to do your hair this morning?" About twenty minutes after Judy arrived, my hair had been trimmed and set, and my Heavenly Father had shown me again that if I will put Him first, He will care for the details—just as He has promised!

Evaluate Your Self-Image

Have you been measuring yourself by the unchanging standard of God's Word or by the accommodating elastic tape measure of comparing yourself with someone else? Maybe you have been using what you believe to be a flaw as a peg on which to hang excuses for not involving yourself in others' lives.

Self-esteem that is too high can be devastating. However, with a servant's heart, we can accept what God made us to be. Pride, not low self-image, is generally our greatest problem. If you were to walk into a room full of people, which of these would you think first: "Who will notice me and come to talk to me?" or "Who is alone and wishing someone would include him or her?" As you answer this question, you will discover a great deal about how you see yourself. Pride asserts itself to believe that someone should notice you and come to you. A servant's heart and acceptance of the way God made you expresses itself by finding someone who needs a friend.

Matthew 22:37–40 tells us, "Jesus said unto him, Thou shalt love the Lord thy God with all thy heart, and with all thy soul, and with all thy mind. This is the first and great commandment. And the second is like unto it, Thou shalt love thy neighbor as thyself...." We do not need to be told to love ourselves. Our *need* is to have the same love for others. Ephesians 5:29 clearly explains our natural self-love: "For no man ever yet hated his own flesh; but nourisheth and cherisheth it, even as the Lord the church."

Second Timothy 3:1–4 declares that being lovers of self instead of lovers of God is one of the indicators of the "last days": "This know also, that in the last days perilous times shall come. For men shall be lovers of their own selves...more than lovers of God."

God's Word has the answer. Psalm 100:3 states: "Know ye that the Lord He is God: it is He that hath made us, and not we ourselves." He has the plan, the pattern, and the provision. Our measuring standard and book of instruction can only be His Word.

Ephesians 1:6 reads: "To the praise of the glory of his grace, wherein he hath made us accepted in the beloved." Could we wish for more? By whom have you wanted to be accepted?

God has not made a mistake. You are what He wanted you to be!

CHOICES

In the Old Testament book of Esther, King Ahasuerus of the Persian Empire was in the third year of his reign. He invited men of importance from all 127 provinces to the palace in Shushan to see his great riches. This festivity lasted 160 days, followed by another seven-day feast for the palace help. During that time, Queen Vashti also had a feast for the women. The king sent a message that Vashti was to come to the men's feast to parade her beauty and her crown.

However, Vashti refused. The king got counsel from his wise men, and they determined that, lest the women of the Persian Empire think this was the way they could treat their husbands, Vashti's royal estate was to be given to another. Therefore, word went out across the provinces to bring beautiful young virgins to the palace to determine who would be the next queen. Among them was Esther, a Jewess who had been adopted by her cousin Mordecai. After a year of preparation and her presentation before King Ahasuerus, Esther was chosen to be queen.

Mordecai often sat at the king's gate. As he was there, he heard two of the king's chamberlains plotting to assassinate King Ahasuerus. Through Esther he sent a warning to the king. Consequently, the two men were hanged, and the king's life was spared.

Wicked Haman was promoted over all the princes in the Persian Empire. Everyone except Mordecai bowed reverently to Haman. Mordecai refused to pay homage to him, and this angered Haman. He spoke to the king and said that he would give ten thousand talents of silver to the treasury of the king if Mordecai and all the Jewish people were killed. The king agreed, and the decree was given. It was sealed with the king's ring of authority and delivered to every province.

Mordecai mourned in sackcloth and ashes. When Esther heard of his mourning, she sent out a change of clothes for him, but Mordecai refused. Instead, he sent word to Esther that she must go to the king to plead for her people, the Jews. Esther had a choice to make, because she knew that anyone entering the inner court of the king could be put to death unless he or she had been summoned by him.

Mordecai said to Esther, "Who knoweth whether thou art come to the kingdom for such a time as this?"

Esther asked her maidens and the Jewish people in Shushan to fast for three days. Then she made her choice: "If I perish, I perish."

The consequences of Esther's choice glorified the Lord and were in His will, and His provision was evident! King Ahasuerus extended his golden scepter to Esther; Mordecai was honored by the king; and Haman was hanged on the gallows he had prepared for Mordecai. The Jewish people were spared!

Had you been Esther, what choice would you have made in response to Mordecai's plea? What would have been the consequences?

What choices have you made today? In light of the choice Esther had to make, our choices seem pretty small: the choice to get up when the alarm rings, what to wear, what to have for breakfast, etc. However, each choice will have ripples of consequences. Let us together consider workable principles by which to make our choices.

Principles for Making Choices

We need to make our choices on the basis of God's Word. In some cases we can take a specific verse and have a specific answer; in others, we must apply a principle from Scripture.

The important key to remember when making a choice is this: always come down on God's side!

Every choice brings with it either positive or negative consequences. The Bible gives countless illustrations of this principle. Joshua is speaking to the Israelites when he tells them in Joshua 24:15, "And if it seem evil unto you to serve the Lord, choose you this day whom ye will serve; whether the gods which your fathers served that were on the other side of the flood, or the gods of the Amorites, in whose land ye dwell: but as for me and my house, we will serve the Lord." He spoke not only for himself, but for his entire household. The consequences of Joshua's choice? After forty years of journeying through the wilderness, Joshua led the Israelites into the promised land!

Eve chose to take the fruit of the tree from which God had clearly told Adam and Eve not to eat. "And when the woman saw that the tree was good for food, and that it was pleasant to the eyes, and a tree to be desired to make one wise, she took of the fruit thereof, and did eat, and gave also unto her husband with her; and he did eat" (Genesis 3:6). You and I know the results of their choice—sin. Romans 5:12 verifies the eternal effects of that choice: "Wherefore, as by one man sin entered into the world, and death by sin; and so death passed upon all men, for that all have sinned." We bear the consequences of that choice: we have all been born sinners. For this, our Lord and Savior Jesus Christ came to die. The greatest choice we make in life is to repent of that sin and ask the Lord Jesus Christ to become our Savior. The consequence is life eternal!

Dorcas, as recorded in Acts 9:36–42, chose to sew clothing for the widows and their children. At the time of her death, she was honored by those to whom she had freely given. Then Dorcas was brought back to life. The consequence? Many trusted Christ as Savior.

Lydia, in Acts 16, chose to open her home for the ministry of hospitality. Paul and Silas and those with them stayed in the home of this new convert. Because of the choices Lydia made, these apostles had a ministry into Europe, where the gospel was spread.

Making a "big choice" is determining to apply principles from the Word of God as the unchanging standard by which the day-by-day choices are then made. For example, we desire to teach our children obedience. God's Word clearly shows us a principle in Ephesians 6:1–4 for that big choice: "Children, obey your parents in the Lord: for this is right. Honor thy father and mother; that it may be well with thee, and thou mayest live long on the earth. And, ye fathers, provoke not your children to wrath: but bring them up in the nurture and admonition of the Lord." Based on that big choice, day-by-day obedience is expected, and day-by-day nurturing is essential. We must apply God's Word and not be dominated by our moods, outside pressures, or circumstances.

The verse I have chosen to use as a reference point for making biblical choices is Matthew 6:33, my life verse: "But seek ye first the kingdom of God, and His righteousness; and all these things shall be added unto you." Examine Matthew 6:33 with me. Then we will look at a practical, workable way to make choices based upon God's Word. "Seek ye first the kingdom of God" (Will it glorify the Lord?); "and His righteousness" (I will choose God's way, not mine. Is it God's will?); "and all these things shall be added unto you" (Will I know the provision of God?).

Will the Choice Glorify the Lord?

The Lord deals with each of us in our present state. He will help us make choices wherever we are. The young mother whose children are in the home all day, whose hours are filled with childhood stories and with directing household traffic, is in far different circumstances from the widow who lives alone or the middle-aged couple whose last child just left the nest. We cannot make our choices based on what someone else is doing. (Review 2 Corinthians 10:12.) They will live with the consequences of their choices just as we will with ours.

Mary and Martha, in their different ways, made choices. Mary chose to sit at the feet of the Lord Jesus and listen as He spoke. Martha chose to busy herself with food preparation when Jesus was in their home. In Luke 10:41–42, the Lord said that Mary had made the better choice: "Martha, Martha, thou art careful and troubled about many things: but one thing is needful; and Mary hath chosen that good part, which shall not be taken away from her." Their choices—and our Lord's reaction to them—show us which the Lord considered more important. As we see with Mary and Martha, many times the choices are not between right and wrong, but between good and best.

Our son-in-law Dennis has been a considerate and sensitive husband to our daughter, Karen. However, they had been married about three years, and their first child, Joshua, was a year old when Dennis was convicted about an area he had taken for granted. He made a big choice during his Bible study in 1 Peter 3:7: "Likewise, ye husbands, dwell with them according to knowledge, giving honor unto the wife, as unto the weaker vessel, and as being heirs together of the grace of life; that your prayers be not hindered." Together they had decided that Karen would be a stay-at-home mom. Dennis realized that he worked at his office at least eight hours a day, and Karen worked at her workplace, their home, during the same hours. His question to himself: "Since we have both labored in the place of God's will for our lives today, should one of us rest in the evening and the other continue working?" He would share responsibilities of their home when he returned from his workplace. He realized that this would glorify the Lord much more, because this was God's will. The consequences? A family doing their separate daily tasks while still working together in the way God led them.

Regarding the choices and consequences honoring purity, young men and young ladies can find instruction from Ephesians 5:25–27: "Husbands, love your wives, even as Christ also loved the church, and gave himself for it; that he might sanctify and cleanse it with the washing of water by the word, That he might present it to himself a glorious church, not having spot, or wrinkle, or any such thing; but that it should be holy and without blemish." The relationship of a husband and wife is to be as the church to Christ. On her wedding day, the bride is to be presented to her bridegroom as spotless and blameless. A young lady who has made the big choice, based upon God's Word, to keep herself pure, knows that she will be presented to her bridegroom spotless and blameless and will enjoy the consequences: freedom from guilt and enjoyment of a life that brings honor to her Savior.

"Just two choices on the shelf: pleasing God or pleasing self" is a saying often used by Dr. Ken Collier, former director of The Wilds Christian Camp and Conference Center in Brevard, North Carolina. When we choose to please self, we glorify self, satisfy our own will, and work out our own provisions. When we choose to please God, we glorify Him, carry out His will, and see His provisions. The consequences, which are sometimes immediate, sometimes future, are dependent on which one we choose to please.

Is the Choice God's Will?

We must seek to know God, not just know about Him. The choices we make are about appropriating His Word to our daily walk. To glorify the Lord in all we do and to know the will of God, we must go to His Word. Even the Lord Jesus often stated that His mission was to do the will of His Father. John 6:38 states: "For I came down from heaven, not to do mine own will, but the will of Him that sent me."

In order to know God's will, we need to have a daily time to be alone with the Lord in His Word and need to have a plan for that time. Then each morning as we make list for the day, we do not have to choose whether or not to have our time with the Lord. That choice has already been made! I have a plan that works well for me. You may want to try it if you do not already have a plan for your personal time with the Lord.

First, begin with a planned memorization project, such as committing a helpful chapter to memory. Begin by reading the chapter several times so that you will clearly understand the content. You may even wish to outline it. Several years ago, I had predetermined that I could not memorize. Then a dear ninety-six-year-old friend, Mrs. Boles, said, "Lorraine, if you say you cannot memorize, you are saying that Psalm 119 is not in the Book."

Psalm 119:11 instructs us: "Thy word have I hid in mine heart, that I might not sin against thee." Determine to learn one verse per week. Read the verse aloud five times each morning. Repeat this process before you go to bed. After you have done this for about three days, you will find that you can recite it without looking at your Bible! Do not begin memorizing verse two until the next week. In the weeks that follow, keep going back over the memorized verses. When you have completed a chapter, be sure that you continue to say it at least once a week for several months. Then go over it at least once a month, and you will have it hidden in your heart forever!

I recall a year when I was given the responsibility for the church Christmas program. Our theme was: "Jesus, the Light of the World." We found a glow-in-the-dark paint and applied it to the large letters displaying the theme across the front of the church. Then, when the lights lowered for the entrance of those portraying the Christmas story, the theme would be displayed clearly for all to see and to remember. In reality, when the lights lowered, the letters were not even visible, much less glowing in the dark. We had not properly read the instructions. In order to make them glow in the dark, they first had to be in the sunlight. Memorization is like that. When there are dark times in our lives, we need the light of God's Word to encourage, strengthen, or challenge us. If we have not been in that light, we are not prepared for the dark times.

Second, ask the Lord to show you something from His Word that will help you glorify Him and strengthen you that day.

Third, read your Bible. At your kitchen table, you can spread out the materials that will make your personal devotions a time of worship, encouragement, and spiritual growth. Do not substitute other books for the Word of God. Use supplemental materials (e.g., a good commentary or other study aids) to help you understand and get the most from the reading of the Word. Second Timothy 2:15 instructs us: "Study to show thyself approved unto God, a workman that needeth not to be ashamed, rightly dividing the word of truth."

Choose a plan for your Bible reading. You may wish to read your Bible through in a year. You may want to do a more in-depth study of one book of the Bible at a time. Character studies are exciting and can be challenging. Word studies are a rich blessing. Have your notebook open (see below) and pen in hand to list references and make notes regarding what you have learned. You will find yourself referring back to these notes many times.

Fourth, have a notebook in which you answer two questions at the end of your Bible reading time. Question one: What did I read today? Question two: What did the Lord show me through what I read? This is your time to meditate upon what you have read and to seek God's wisdom on how to apply it to your life. Answer each of the questions with only one or two sentences. Making your answers too long or detailed will discourage you from consistently using the notebook.

Fifth is your prayer time. Have a prayer list. Perhaps you could take one page of your notebook and line it into seven columns, one for each day of the week. Simply list those for whom you wish to pray each day. If you have promised to pray for someone, write it down so that you will not forget. Often we meet friends who tell us that they pray for us on a given day of every week. What an encouragement! My dear friend, Lillian, told me that she prayed for us each time she kneaded her sourdough bread. (She got her first sourdough starter from me, so it was one of our common bonds.) It doesn't just happen. It is a plan. You may wish to take the pages following your prayer list to record praises and answers to prayer. First Thessalonians 5:16–18 tells us to "Rejoice evermore. Pray without ceasing. In everything give thanks: for this is the will of God in Christ Jesus concerning you."

I recommend that you keep some little sticky notes in the front of your Bible. When you learn of something for which you should pray, write it on one of the notes. Later, transfer the note to your prayer list and pray for that need.

Our daily devotions should be the highlight of our day! Never let them become a boring ritual. Psalm 119:105 states: "Thy word is a lamp unto my feet, and a light unto my path." If we are to glorify God and be in His will, surely we must choose to use the light of His Word for every choice we make.

Will the Provision Be from the Lord?

Our Lord Jesus knew the provision of God the Father. He tells us in John 16:15: "All things that the Father hath are mine." Instead of the quest for earthly provisions, our Lord sought to glorify His Father, carry out His will, and then rest in the provision of His Father. How often do we spend so much time pursuing what we think we need for our present life that we spend little time pursuing what our Lord wishes to provide for us? In allowing Him to provide, we glorify Him!

Solomon is a picture of what God is telling us in Matthew 6:33. Solomon chose to ask God for wisdom that he might rule his people well. He sought the mind of God, not material possessions. We read in 2 Chronicles 1:11–12: "And God said to Solomon, 'Because this was in thine heart, and thou hast not asked riches, wealth, or honor, nor the life of thine enemies, neither yet hast asked long life; but hast asked wisdom and knowledge for thyself, that thou mayest judge my people, over whom I have made thee king: wisdom and knowledge is granted unto thee; and I will give thee riches, and wealth, and honor, such as none of the kings have had that have been before thee, neither shall there any after thee have the like.'" Solomon's choice brought monumental consequences: the Lord was glorified; His will was clear; and His provision was abundant beyond belief!

Do we allow God's provision of grace in times of testing? How do we choose to react when someone has accused us falsely or broken a promise? If we choose to dwell on the hurt, the consequences are spelled out in Hebrews 12:15: "Looking diligently lest any man fail of the grace of God; lest any root of bitterness springing up trouble you, and thereby many be defiled." Our bitter spirits will not only defile *our* lives but also the lives of others, including our children. Instead, if we commit the testing to the Lord and rejoice in His grace, the consequences are described in 2 Corinthians 1:3–4, "Blessed be God, even the Father of our Lord Jesus Christ, the Father of mercies, and the God of all comfort; Who comforteth us in all our tribulation, that we may be able to comfort them which are in any trouble, by the comfort wherewith we ourselves are comforted of God." Our Lord is glorified; His will is accomplished; and His provision is realized.

The Principle of Choice in Forgiving

Let's look at Joseph in the book of Genesis. His Jewish brothers sold him to Ishmeelite traders who were going from Gilead down to Egypt. Joseph must have been terrified! Later, Joseph was cast into prison, because the wife of his Egyptian master lied about Joseph's conduct. While in prison, he was promised by the butler, whose dream Joseph interpreted, that he would plead Joseph's cause to Pharaoh when he got out of prison. However, the butler did not keep his promise. Yet through all of this, Joseph chose to forgive each one who had wronged him. The results were positive. His brothers came to Egypt seeking food, and Joseph was the one to provide it. He could say in Genesis 50:19–20, "Fear not: for am I in the place of God? But as for you, ye thought evil against me; but God meant it unto good, to bring to pass, as it is this day, to save much people alive." Joseph is one of my Bible heroes! He chose to leave the punishing to God, and he chose to forgive. The consequences were definitely positive: the preserving of the people of Israel, God's chosen people!

The choice to forgive when we are stinging from an offense is among the hardest to make. The following story, taken from *First We Have Coffee*, by Margaret Jensen, was used by permission.

Not long before her death, the Norwegian grandmother, Ella Tweten, was visited by her daughter and granddaughter. Janice, the granddaughter, heard Grandma saying, "Love and forgive. Love and forgive." She then quoted Mark 11:25: "And when ye stand praying, forgive, if ye have ought against any: that your Father also which is in heaven may forgive you your trespasses." Janice said that there were some things she could not forgive, which prompted a story by Grandma Tweten.

"I'll tell you about two people whom I will call John and Mary." John was a preacher, and Mary was his wife. Any money they could save was spent on books for John's ministry.

In addition to the money for books, Mary saved until she could buy a much-needed new lamp for John and some material for a pretty new spring dress for herself. She made a soft, billowing, voile dress with lace around the neck and sleeves and a big sash. Instead of putting her hair into a tight bun on top of her head, she let it hang freely down her back. The twenty-three-year-old preacher's wife was wearing her pretty new spring dress when John came in. He looked at Mary, and like a flash of summer lightning said, "Money for foolishness! No libraries, no books, no one to talk to...." In his rage, he ripped Mary's billowing spring dress into shreds and then rode off to unleash the remainder of his anger.

Mary took the shredded dress and folded it into a small package and put it into her trunk. The storm had passed, but much debris had been left behind. Life went on as usual, but the song was gone from Mary's heart.

Pastor Hansen was coming to preach for their church one Sunday, and Mary thought she could finally talk to someone about her burden. Sunday morning, Pastor Hansen announced his text: Mark 11:25. He said that forgiveness was not a feeling, but an act of faith. It was a choice, a definite act of the will, in clear obedience to God's command. Mary thought she could never forget what had happened. Pastor Hansen said that God's love and His forgiveness could and would cushion the memory until the imprint was gone. He added the when you forgive, you must destroy the evidence and remember only to love.

After church Mary served dinner to John and Pastor Hansen. Mary knew what she had to do—destroy the evidence. She opened the trunk, got out the rolled-up dress, and lifted the lid on the wood-burning stove.

As she threw in the once-beautiful, now-tattered dress, John walked in and asked, "Mary, what are you doing?"

Mary's sobs and trembling abated long enough to say, "Destroying the evidence."

John remembered what had happened and asked, "Mary, will you please forgive me?"

Grandma Ella said, "Now John has gone home. Fifty-eight years together, and I miss him." Janet then realized that the story was about Grandma Ella Tweten and Grandpa Tweten, who was now with the Lord.

She had made a wise choice. She had enjoyed the consequences of that choice for fifty-eight years. Her children and grandchildren would continue to enjoy the benefits of her choice.

Teaching Our Children How to Make Choices

As parents, we are the primary models for teaching our children how to make choices. They see us making the big choices, then day-by-day and moment-by-moment choices based on those big choices. It doesn't take long for a child to know if those choices are made from a foundation that is solid and stable or one that changes according to the mood of the moment. They also see us living with the results of those choices.

In his book *If I Perish, I Perish*, published by Torchbearers, Major W. Ian Thomas speaks of house-training a puppy. When that fluffy little puppy dines upon the steak about to be prepared for the family, he gets a smack. He has done wrong. When the puppy obeys the command to sit on his hind legs and stick out his paws, he gets candy. He has done right. In the house-training process, the puppy discovers that every earnest attempt receives its due reward. He learns that there are not only things in life that are "smack wrong," but there are things in life that are "candy right"—not right because they are right, but they are simply right because they get a reward. The puppy chooses to behave, based on the consequences he wishes to receive: a smack or candy. The puppy has no moral or spiritual convictions determining his choices. He has simply been house-trained.

Major Thomas goes on to say that many young people who profess to be Christians, whose conduct conforms to prescribed patterns, have been evangelically house-trained. They have not established biblical convictions. When they are detached from their training grounds (home, church, Christian school), they will head for disaster, because their choices have been made on the basis of "smack wrong" or "candy right," not on God's Word.

We must teach our children to make choices on the basis of God's Word. Do they see us using God's Word as our guide, making choices that glorify the Lord, living in His will, and allowing Him to supply the provisions?

Even a small child must know that choices have consequences: some that bring joy and some that bring sorrow. Choosing not to be ready at the appointed time will cause the whole family to be late. Choosing not to prepare for a test will mean a lower grade. Choosing to help with household chores will allow time for family fun or playtime with friends. Making wise choices about use of allowance money will mean that there is enough to buy a desired item.

When bringing up our children, we are faced with the reality of another dimension of the effect of every choice we make. Proverbs 23:26 counsels us: "My son, give me thine heart, and let thine eyes observe my ways." This same thought is underscored in a familiar saying: "Your walk talks, and your talk talks, but your walk talks louder than your talk talks."

As we seek to do the will of God as one who desires to glorify the Lord, we can be assured of the provision of God. Our choices are made, not as a child who makes them with the pleasure of the moment in mind, but as an adult. First Corinthians 13:11 challenges our choice-making: "When I was a child, I spake as a child, I understood as a child, I thought as a child: but when I became a man, I put away childish things." Have you ever played checkers with a little child? He or she sees only the immediate choice, which may be jumping one of your checkers. However, the child may not see the consequence of that choice: that you will get to jump three of his or her checkers!

Lot chose the well-watered plains of Jordan when his uncle Abraham gave him a choice. Like a child, he chose what looked good at the moment. He pitched his tent toward Sodom. His choice brought heartache. He lost his wife when she chose to disobey the angel's warning to flee and not look back. He escaped to the mountains, where his two daughters made him drink wine, then both became pregnant by their father. Out of this choice came Moab, born to the elder daughter, and Ammon, born to the younger. The Moabites and Ammonites were archenemies of the Jewish people. Lot's choices were made with the satisfaction of the moment in mind, not the long-term view of the consequences of those choices. Look at the negative consequences that resulted!

Second Corinthians 4:17–18 reminds us: "For our light affliction, which is but for a moment, worketh for us a far more exceeding and eternal weight of glory; while we look not at the things which are seen, but at the things which are not seen: for the things which are seen are temporal; but the things which are not seen are eternal." It is not always easy to make right choices. It is easy to look at the temporal—the here and now—and covet the temporary benefits. We need to stop and think that there are consequences from the decision we are about to make.

Our neighbors in Minnesota were a young couple with three children. One morning, I saw Janet making a good choice. She was painting a shelf out in their yard. I commented on her project, and her answer was a delight! "When I wash clothes, feed babies, and read kiddie stories much of the day, I sometimes need to do something for somebody over three feet tall. Today I am cleaning the closet and giving the shelves a fresh coat of paint." Janet had made a good choice! She knew that renewing her vitality by temporarily changing her focus would be rewarding to her whole family.

Conclusion

God created us with the privilege of making choices. If something unexpected happens, do we let it irritate us and use it as an excuse for a disrupted and unproductive life? How much better to choose to glorify the Lord, know His will, and enjoy His provision. When we make the big choice to apply God's Word in each area of our lives, we can make those moment-by-moment choices with far greater confidence.

Deuteronomy 30:19 tells us that God said to the Israelites, "I call heaven and earth to record this day against you, that I have set before you life and death, blessing and cursing: therefore choose life, that both thou and thy seed may live." We and our seed (that is, our children) will bear the consequences of our choices. Therefore our big choices about the issues of life must be made prayerfully and on the basis of God's Word. As we make choices every day—whether about obedience, friends, role models, college, our life's companion, submission, our daily routine—do our decisions glorify the Lord? Are they the will of God? Will the result of those decisions be the provision of God?

Esther had a difficult choice to make. It was one that could have cost her life. Mordecai warned her that she might have come to the kingdom "for such a time as this." What a responsibility! The same God who led Esther in her choice desires to guide you and me as we make our choices.

Matthew 6:33 will guide us in the choices we must make: "But seek ye first the kingdom of God, and his righteousness; and all these things shall be added unto you." May our desire always be to glorify the Lord, do His will, and see His provision!

DEATH OF A DREAM

It was about midnight when our phone rang. Donna was on the phone, asking that we please come to her home, because Carl was having a difficult time. He had just received word that the position he had held for eighteen years would no longer be his in another two months.

When we arrived, Carl, usually an extrovert and a communicative person, was slumped into a chair in the corner of the living room. Their two children were already sleeping soundly, but no sleep would come to Carl and Donna. Donna had asked Carl if she could call my husband, Ben, who was their pastor. She was confident that Ben would share their heartache and help them find some hope and encouragement from God's Word.

After being in their home for about an hour, we could see that Carl was at rock bottom physically, emotionally, and even spiritually. What we were seeing was exactly what we had seen when a loved one was taken in death.

So I said to Donna, "Do you realize that Carl's reaction to this is just like someone who has lost the person dearest to him or her in death?"

Donna's answer was, "Lorraine, this has been the *death of a dream*."

That night, we realized that being engulfed in the debris of a shattered dream unleashes every emotion and stage faced by someone mourning a death. Therefore, the understanding and encouragement so needed by someone who is mourning the death of a loved one is also vital for the one who has had the death of a dream.

First Thessalonians 4:13, speaking of believers who have died—and to those who grieve their absence—says: "But I would not have you to be ignorant, brethren, concerning them who are asleep, that ye sorrow not, even as others who have no hope." When there has been the death of a loved one, or a dream, we will sorrow. But our comfort comes in knowing that yes, we sorrow—but not as those who have no hope.

The Death of a Dream

Suppose someone rushed to you and said, "We just got a call that your husband (your child, your mother, the person dearest to you) passed away." Would you be prepared to cope with that? Suppose the abdominal pain you have been having has gotten enough worse in the last few months that you have finally agreed to go to the doctor. He says that you must have surgery. After surgery, you hear the much-feared words: "I am sorry, but there is nothing we can do—you probably have three to four months left." Are you prepared to cope with that?

You learn that your mate of forty years has Alzheimer's. Are you prepared to cope with that? Your teenage daughter is weeping uncontrollably in her room. You go in, and she falls into your arms, crying out, "Mom, I think I'm pregnant." Are you prepared to cope with that? Your husband of seven years tells you that your marriage is finished. He has finally found the "right" person, and he is leaving you. Would you be prepared to cope with that?

Rarely do people cope with their plight the way they think they would. The person who is an extrovert and who is happy-go-lucky often finds it impossible to communicate his or her feelings. Conversely, the normally quiet, sedate person becomes loud or unusually verbal in his or her expressions. You cannot plan on how you will react. Your security in the Lord Jesus Christ as Savior, your consistent time in God's Word, and a life yielded to bringing honor to the Lord are the best preparations for whatever comes into your life.

Stages of Grief and Coping

When there has been the death of a loved one or the death of a dream, most people go through several different stages. Some may go through them very quickly. For others, it may take a matter of years before getting to the final stage.

This is not the time to follow what others believe you should do. You must discover your own needs and your own manner of dealing with them.

Shock or Anesthesia

Stage one occurs after you have had a severe shock. You realize something overwhelming has happened to someone. It is as though you are in a plastic bubble. You realize it has happened—but not that it has happened to you. You have not yet allowed yourself to comprehend the reality.

Emotional Expression

The second stage is that of emotional expression. One person may begin screaming, have an outpouring of tears, and just fall apart. The person who is normally the extrovert may become very quiet, simply expressing, "No, this cannot be."

In her book, *Roses in December*, Marilyn Willett Heavilin writes: "Between 75 and 85 percent of the couples who lose a child will divorce within the first five years after the death." Each is reacting to grief in a manner inconsistent with his or her usual behavior. Suddenly, it seems like they are strangers.

Depression and Loneliness

The period of depression and loneliness may vary. During this time, you tend to focus on your own bereavement. "I am without a mate (job, honor, health, something precious to me)."

Physical Distress Symptoms

You may experience a myriad of physical distress symptoms. When someone is not aware of what is happening, he or she may be too embarrassed and ashamed to tell anyone. One of our older ladies at church shared with a close friend that she was often awakened at night by what seemed like the presence of her deceased husband. He had been a pastor. She would see him standing at the foot of her bed, dressed, ready to preach, and holding his Bible in his hand. She would look at him as long as she could, then she would reach out to touch him, but he was not there. Her words to her friend were: "Don't tell anyone else, because they will think I am losing my mind." What a sad commentary on those of us as her church family that she did not believe that we would understand.

Women who are alone following a divorce have shared with me that they have sensed the presence of their former husband on the other side of the bed, but they were too embarrassed to share that with anyone. They had no idea that others have had the same experience.

With some, there is a loss of weight and appetite, because they are filled with distress. Food feels like cotton; it can be chewed, but it cannot be swallowed. Some say food tastes bitter. With others, the only comfort—because of the emptiness they are experiencing—is found in eating. Therefore, for that person, there will be weight gain.

Tightness of chest muscles is frequently present: a feeling that one simply cannot get his or her breath or that a wide rubber band is being pulled so tightly that his or her chest will burst. How often have we heard of a widow of six weeks who was rushed to the hospital with an apparent heart attack? Though tests showed that this was not happening, the symptoms were there.

Many experience an inability to concentrate on even simple tasks. I recall a friend sharing that following her sister's death, some friends were coming over for coffee. She was going to serve a simple coffee cake that she and her mother had made since she was a little girl. It contained six ingredients; she had never even written the recipe down—she had just known it. That morning, to save her life, she could not remember how to make the coffee cake. It embarrassed her to realize that she could not recall something so basic. She called her husband, and he picked up a commercial coffee cake for her to serve her friends.

Another physical symptom that is not unusual during this period is the inability to sleep. Often, the person is afraid to go to sleep because of the fear of the dreams that may occur. In the quietness of being alone, there are sometimes memories that flood the heart and mind.

The person may cry very easily. The triggering of a memory may cause an uncontrollable outburst of crying. I recall a lady who was attending a "singspiration" at our home. When we started a hymn that had been precious to her deceased son, she began crying. A blessing to all who were aware of it was when we saw her husband reach over and give her a warm, understanding hug. She came to me later and apologized for what had happened and shared her embarrassment. I told her that we loved her, and that we understood. We were all deeply touched by her longing mother's heart.

Panic or Fear

There is often a sense of guilt over the loss that has occurred. Children of a divorced couple frequently have this fear.

I recall a neighbor lady whom we had the privilege of leading to the Lord following her divorce. I was having a weekly Bible study with her to help her grow in her new faith in Christ. One morning, I asked Carol if her eight-year-old, Jeff, had ever said to her that he believed he had caused their divorce.

Carol said, "Not until last night." The night before our conversation, Jeff disobeyed her. She shouted at him. He shouted back that it was just like the night his daddy had left the house and had not come back.

Jeff said, "I spilled my milk, and you screamed at me. Daddy screamed at you for screaming at me; then Daddy left and did not come back. I know it's all my fault that he won't ever come back to live with us."

That eight-year-old had been carrying a pretty heavy load during those months. Carol told him that he was not the cause; the problem had been between his mom and dad.

When someone is taken in death because of an extended illness, you may experience a sense of guilt, because you did not insist that the person go to the doctor much earlier. However, always remember: the decision you made at that time was based on the information you had.

Hostility or Resentment

Anger regarding what has happened can overwhelm you. You may even feel this as anger toward the person who died or toward the one to whom this difficulty has come. You wonder: "How could you have let such a thing happen?" or "Don't you see what you have done to me?" This is often when we ask: "Why?" It's not wrong to ask why—to consider all that has taken place. However, hostility—even toward God—can develop if we are simply looking for someone to blame.

Inability to Return to Normal

This is when you hit rock bottom. It seems that life will never be the same again. There is a sense of insecurity that your world will never again return to normal.

Hope Returning

Spring follows winter. God is in control, so we need not fear.

Reality Must Be Confirmed

Finally, there is a struggle within to confirm reality. This *has* happened. Life *will* go on. It is *not* the end. You *must* regroup. In the process, you have grieved the past, the present, and what might have been the future.

***

No two people will spend the same amount of time in any of the stages. We can never judge another person's experience by our own. I recall a young husband whose wife died, leaving him with three young children. He handled them with such dignity and assurance that he amazed everyone close to him. About two years after his wife's death, he began having a very difficult time, and his stability seemed to evaporate. He said that he believed his friends had stopped praying for him. His solitude and awesome sense of responsibility began to overwhelm him. Thankfully, friends helped him through the time of despair, and he was able to accept what had happened. We soon saw him go forward with a new assurance of the Lord's guidance for his life.

Sometimes, a death that is sudden increases the intensity of the stages of grief. When there has been a prolonged illness or an anticipation of the loss, some of the stages have already been experienced before the actual loss even occurs.

Surety of God's Care

The ever-present care of a loving Savior is the anchor of our hope through the uncertain waters of the present and future. Hopefully, our church family and friends have been very helpful and supportive during the early time of our grieving, but we must avoid becoming comfortable in our grief. A charming seventy-eight-year-old lady said to me, "My husband of fifty years had been dead for two years when I had to decide, 'Was I going to wallow in my widowhood for the rest of my life, or was I going to start serving the Lord?'" First Corinthians 10:13 says, "There hath no temptation taken you but such as is common to man: but God is faithful, who will not suffer you to be tempted above that ye are able; but will with the temptation also make a way to escape, that ye may be able to bear it." God is faithful. He knows of your broken heart, and He tells you in 1 Peter 5:7: "Casting all your care upon Him, for He careth for you."

I believe that our choice to resent what has happened or to go on and give God the glory relates to how we handle the "why" of our grief. Has it been, "Why me, Lord?" If so, we are likely going to go through some time of resentment. However, if we can honestly say: "Lord, why did You entrust this to me?"—seeking to honor Him through what happened—we will lean upon Him to guide us.

Second Corinthians 1:3–4 exhorts us: "Blessed be God, even the Father of our Lord Jesus Christ, the Father of mercies, and the God of all comfort; Who comforteth us in all our tribulation, that we may be able to comfort them that are in any trouble, by the comfort wherewith we ourselves are comforted of God." Be sure to mark that well in your Bible.

Sometimes, God permits us to sorrow so that we may allow Him to comfort us. Therefore, when others need comforting, we can comfort them with the same comfort with which we have been comforted. Often, those who have gone through the deepest water are the ones who are the greatest source of encouragement and comfort in a time of grief. God wants you to have a comforting ministry to others. One of your greatest sources of comfort and self-worth is realizing that God wants to use you—and what has happened to you—to encourage others who may be encountering the same dark path you walked. God has not forsaken you.

This is such an important time to be faithful in your daily time with the Lord. (On pages 62–66, I shared my personal plan for spending time in His Word.)

Surrender to God's Choice

You must surrender to God's choice and avoid the possibility of any resentment. Could this have happened for God's glory? Can you commit it to the God of all comfort?

If you have experienced the death of a dream, you have passed through the same steps experienced by someone who has lost a loved one in death. Review the ten stages of grief. If this is like a death, what should there be following a death? There has to be a burial, doesn't there? We know that when a loved one dies, there is a funeral; this is followed by a gracious and loving burial of the body. Many times, when there is the death of a dream (the lost job, relationship, health, security), we carry the corpse of that dead dream with us—refusing to bury it—and it begins to have a stench.

Philippians 4:4 tells us, "Rejoice in the Lord always, and again I say rejoice." God would not have instructed us to do this if it were not possible. If we can rejoice in the Lord always—even with a broken heart—then, we are ready to go on and to do so without resentment.

Resentment is a strong sense of anger or displeasure. All through life, we must hold lightly to those people and those things that God has allowed us to share. How do we view our relationships with our children, our job, our spouse, or our health? Do we believe that we own them? What we own, we clutch tenaciously. When taken from us, some of its flesh remains under our fingernails. God has loaned us our families, our jobs, and our health, and we have the joyous privilege of caring for them and guarding them for the real Owner: God Himself. We cannot allow resentment to consume us. Our Lord has graciously allowed us to care for someone or something that He has loaned to us.

As I view it, when the thought of the empty nest is all-consuming, it becomes a clear example of a parent believing that he or she owns a child. When that child marries and moves away from the home, there is a sense that something which was owned has been snatched away. Psalm 127:3 says, "Lo, children are an heritage of the Lord." We have simply been caring for them for the real Owner. Our children were on loan to us.

In fact, our bodies are on loan to us. God's Word tells us that our bodies are the temple of the Holy Spirit (1 Corinthians 6:19–20). A temple does not have a co-owner. We are tenting there as long as the Owner wills. We take care of our bodies to glorify the Lord. That knowledge makes all the difference in the world in our attitudes.

A few years ago, our daughter Brenda went through the death of a dream. With everything prepared for her upcoming wedding, there was suddenly a broken engagement. Brenda's family and friends encouraged her and shared her heartache. Outwardly, it seemed that she was doing well. One evening, just two weeks later, when we called her, we heard the bubbly, pleasant-voiced Brenda that we had not heard since the death of her dream.

She told us, "Today, my apartment mate said something that brought together all the Scripture and advice that has been shared with me. Andrea said, 'I grew up in California, and it was there I learned that most of the fruit grows in the valleys.'"

The valley through which Brenda had passed could now be viewed from a new perspective—as a time for fruit-bearing. All too often, we like the mountain-top experiences and shun the valleys. However, it is often the time in the valley that causes us to realize that our sufficiency is from the Lord.

You cannot live in the past. Your past can consume your present and your future if you allow it to happen. If your death of a dream has caused you to harbor bitterness against someone, you have made yourself a slave to that person. There are places you cannot go and things you cannot do because of that bitterness.

Think through the stages of grief. What choices will you make? Will you regroup or resent? If you allow bitterness and resentment to come into your life, you—and also many others—will be affected. Hebrews 12:15 states: "Looking diligently lest any man fail of the grace of God; lest any root of bitterness springing up trouble you, and thereby many be defiled." Take care of any bitterness that has flooded your life because of the death of your dream. It may be something you need to settle with the Lord. Possibly, there is a person from whom you need to ask forgiveness. There may be someone against whom you have been bitter. Take care of it now.

If you find yourself walking through the valley of the death of a dream, I trust that you will emerge a stronger, more fruitful person.

Perhaps you have just read this book, and you are now aware of your need for this loving Savior. Trust Him today!

Romans 3:10: "There is none righteous, no, not one."

Romans 3:23: "For all have sinned, and come short of the glory of God."

Romans 6:23: "For the wages of sin is death; but the gift of God is eternal life through Jesus Christ our Lord."

Romans 5:8: "But God commendeth His love toward us, in that, while we were yet sinners, Christ died for us."

Romans 10:9–10: "That if thou shalt confess with thy mouth the Lord Jesus, and shalt believe in thine heart that God hath raised Him from the dead, thou shalt be saved. For with the heart man believeth unto righteousness; and with the mouth confession is made unto salvation."

Place your faith in the Lord Jesus Christ as your own personal Savior. Seek out a Bible-believing friend or pastor to help you grow in your newfound faith. Life is short. Eternity is forever.

ABOUT THE AUTHOR

Lorraine Strohbehn grew up on a farm in the southwestern corner of Wisconsin and graduated from Methodist Hospital School of Nursing in Madison, Wisconsin. As the wife of a pastor, with all of its many facets, Lorraine has served the Lord as a teacher of women's classes, as a conference, retreat, and banquet speaker, as a Bible study leader, and as an author. For over twenty years, she shared with her husband, Dr. Ben Strohbehn (deceased 2015), in their family conference ministry across the United States and around the world. Lorraine is the mother of four children, grandmother of four, and great-grandmother of two.

Please visit www.petalsfromthebasket.com for additional books available by Ben Strohbehn, Lorraine Strohbehn, and Brenda Strohbehn.

You may contact Lorraine Strohbehn at:
Grandma@PetalsfromtheBasket.com

Made in the USA
San Bernardino, CA
22 March 2016